Johann Sebastian Bach

Cello Suites No's 1-6

BWV 1007
BWV 1008
BWV 1009
BWV 1010
BWV 1011
BWV 1012

A Score for the Cello

Copyright © 2011 Read Books Ltd.
This book is copyright and may not be
reproduced or copied in any way without
the express permission of the publisher in writing

British Library Cataloguing-in-Publication Data
A catalogue record for this book is available from
the British Library

SUITE I.

Prélude.

Allemande.

Courante.

Sarabande.

Menuet I.

Menuet II.

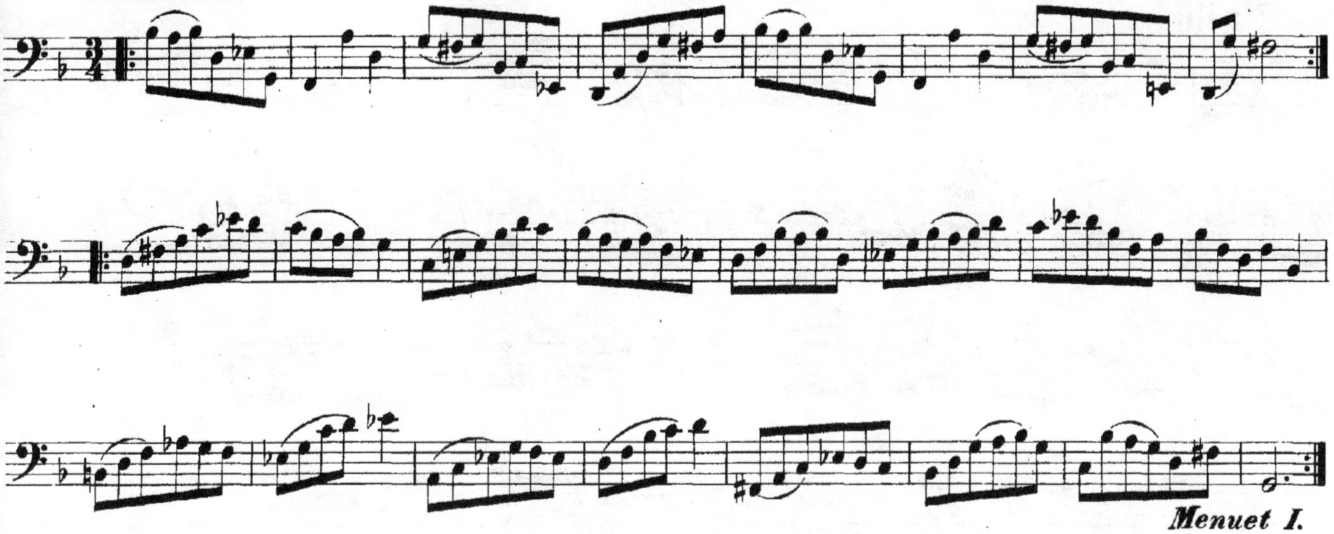

Menuet I.
da Capo.

Gigue.

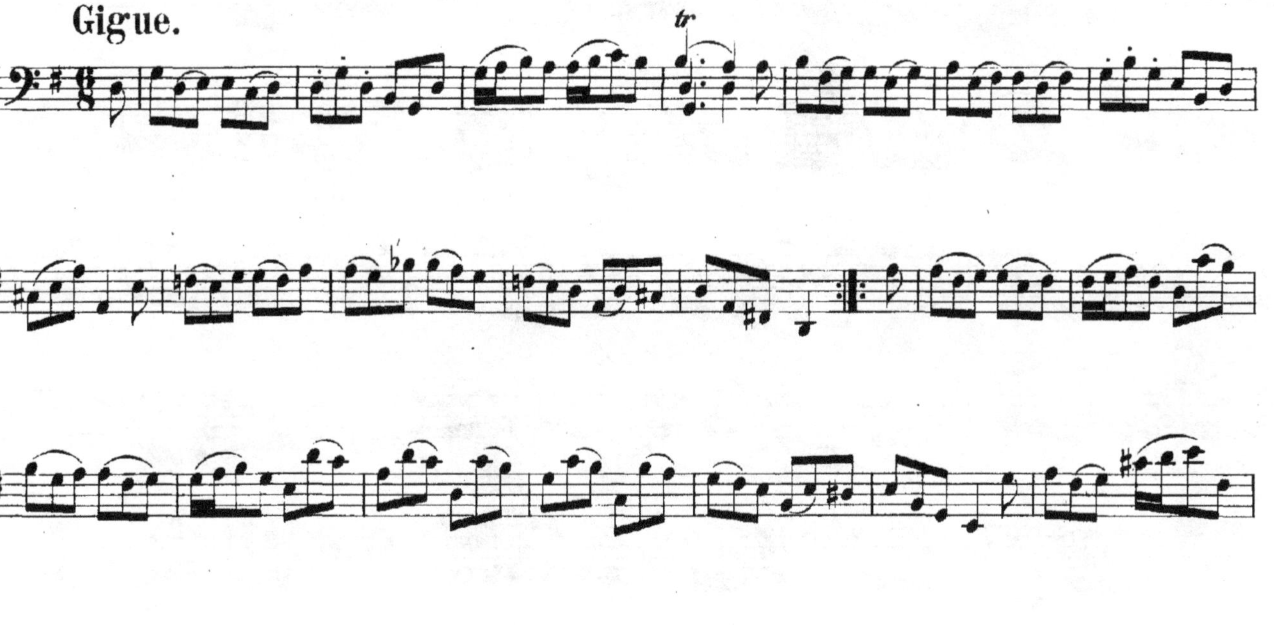

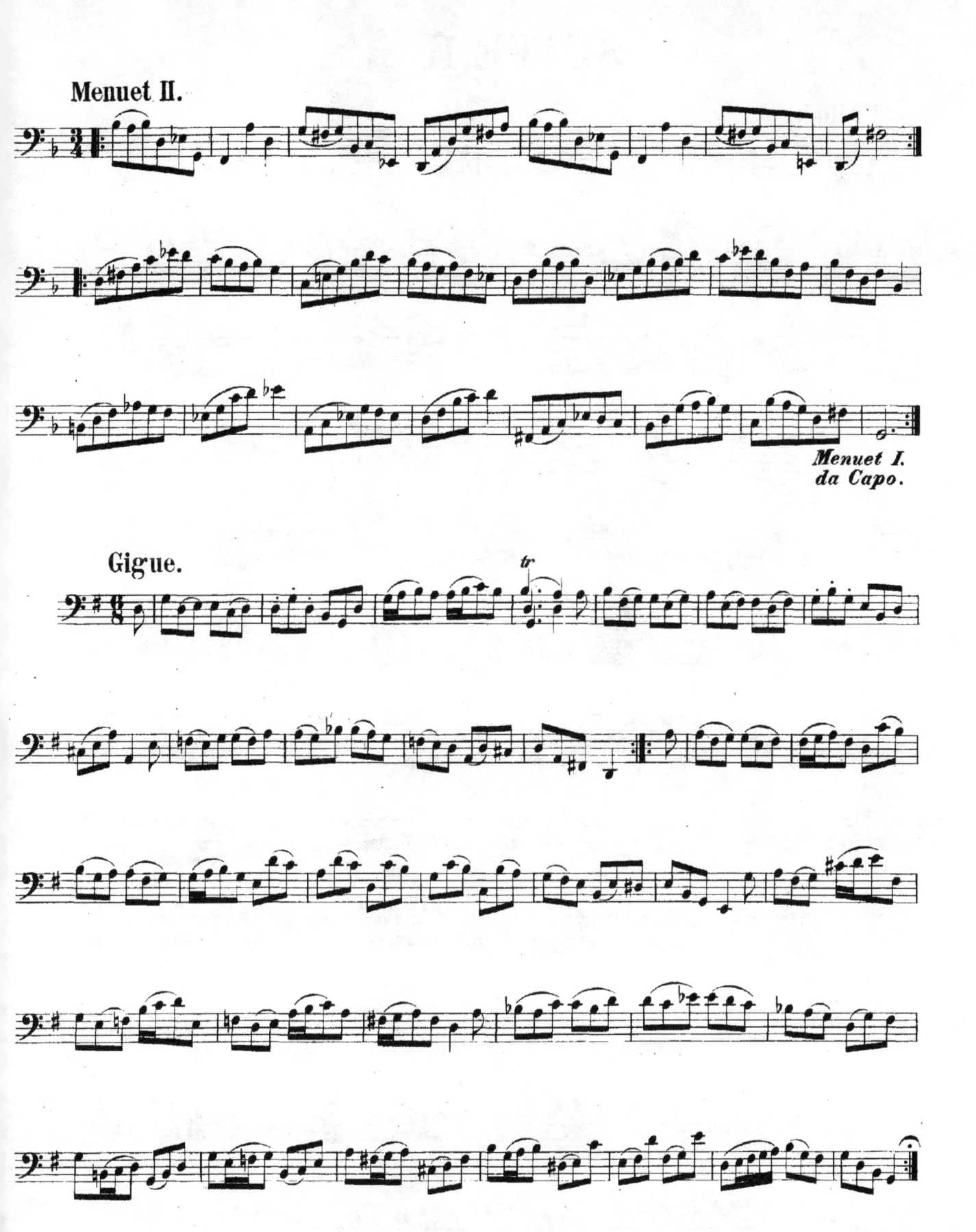

SUITE II.

Prélude.

Allemande.

Courante.

Sarabande.

Menuet I.

Menuet II.

Menuet I. da Capo.

Gigue.

SUITE III.

Prélude.

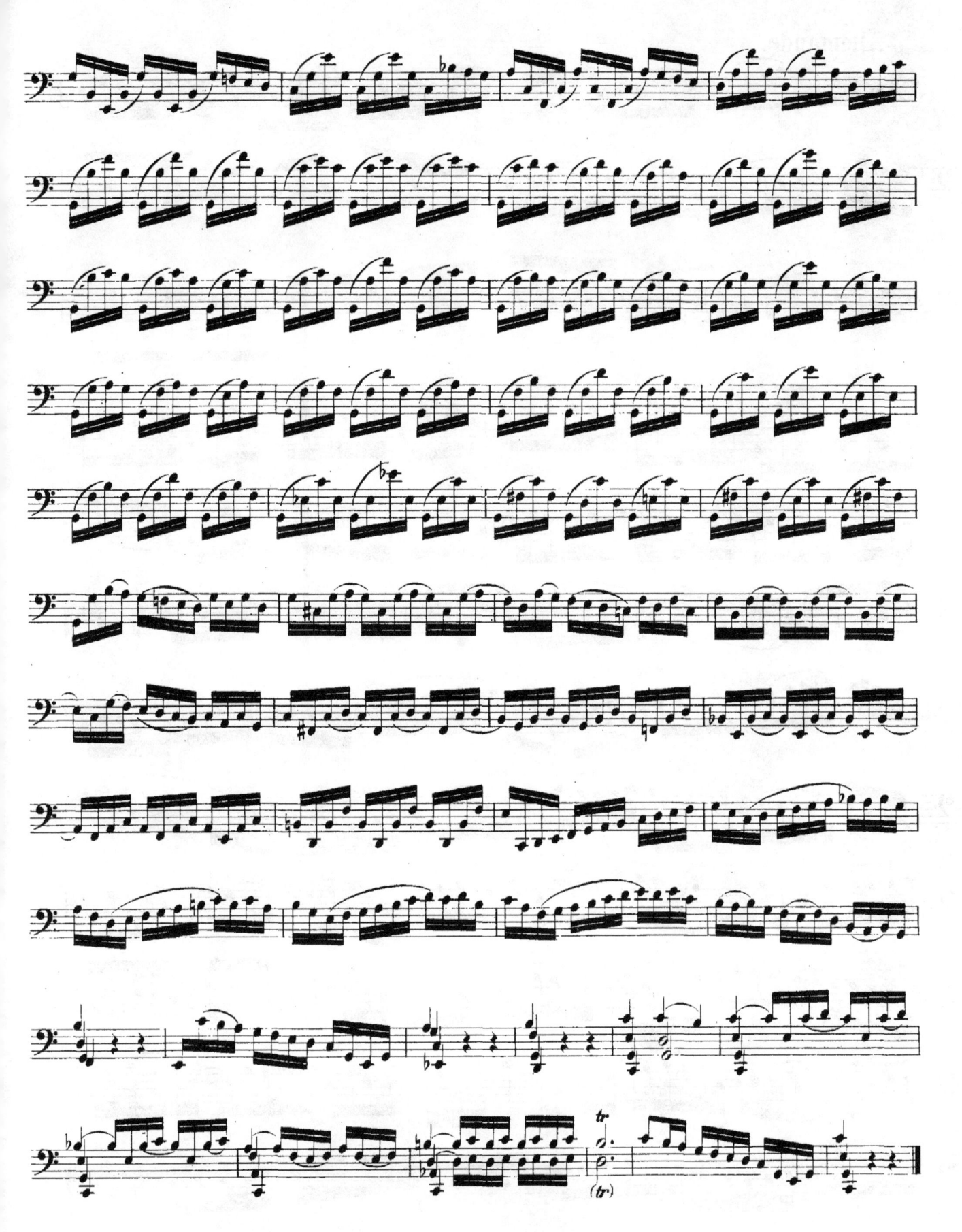

B. W. XXVII.(1)

Allemande.

Courante.

Sarabande.

Bourrée I.

Bourrée II.

piano

Bourrée I. da Capo.

Gigue.

SUITE IV.

Prélude.

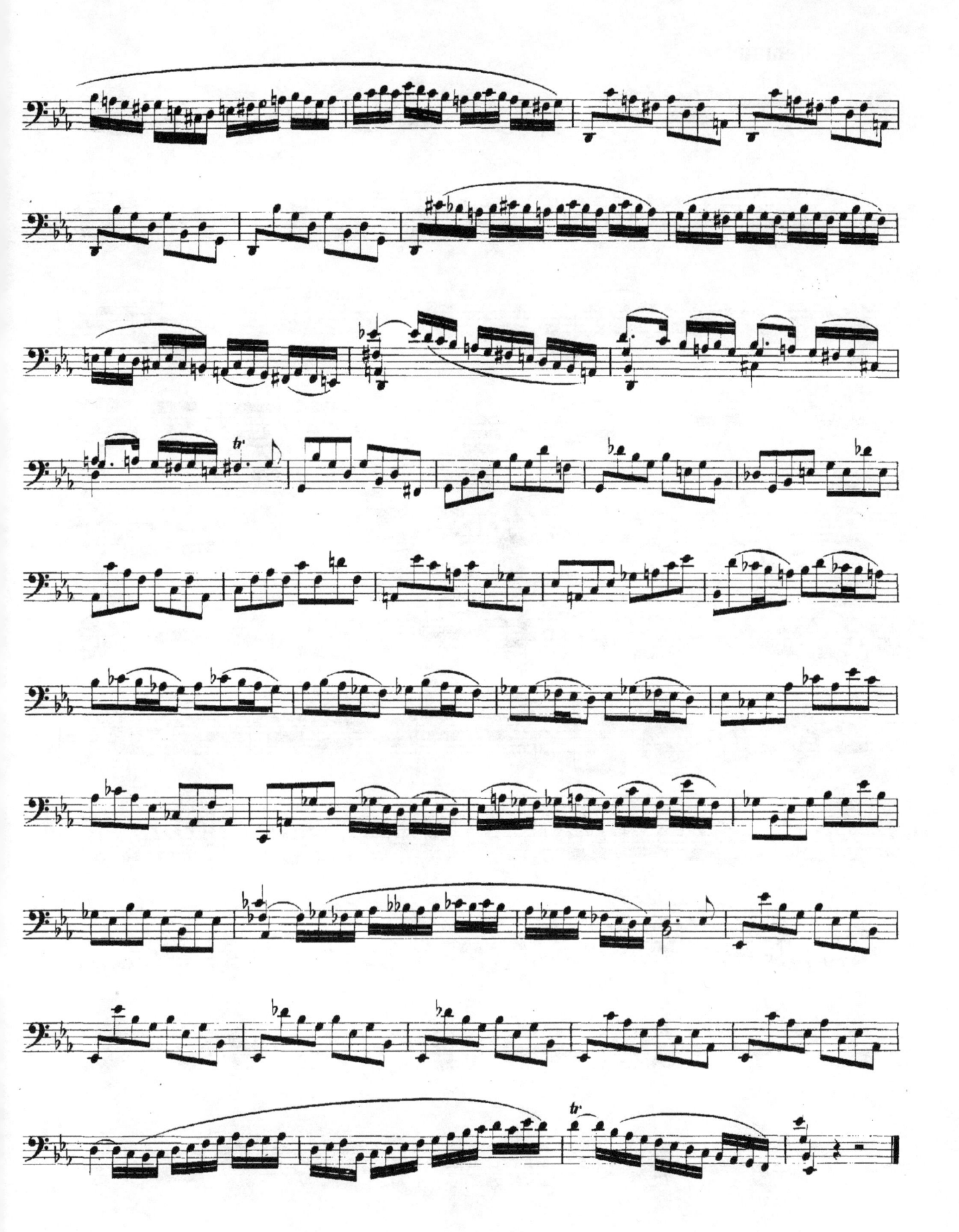

B.W. XXVII.(1)

Allemande.

Courante.

Sarabande.

Bourrée I.

Bourrée II.

Bourrée I.
da Capo.

Gigue.

SUITE V.

Discordant. Accord:

Prélude.

*) Über die, hier genau nach der Berliner Originalvorlage wiedergegebene
Notirungsweise dieser Suite enthält das Vorwort nähere Mittheilung.

B.W. XXVII.(1)

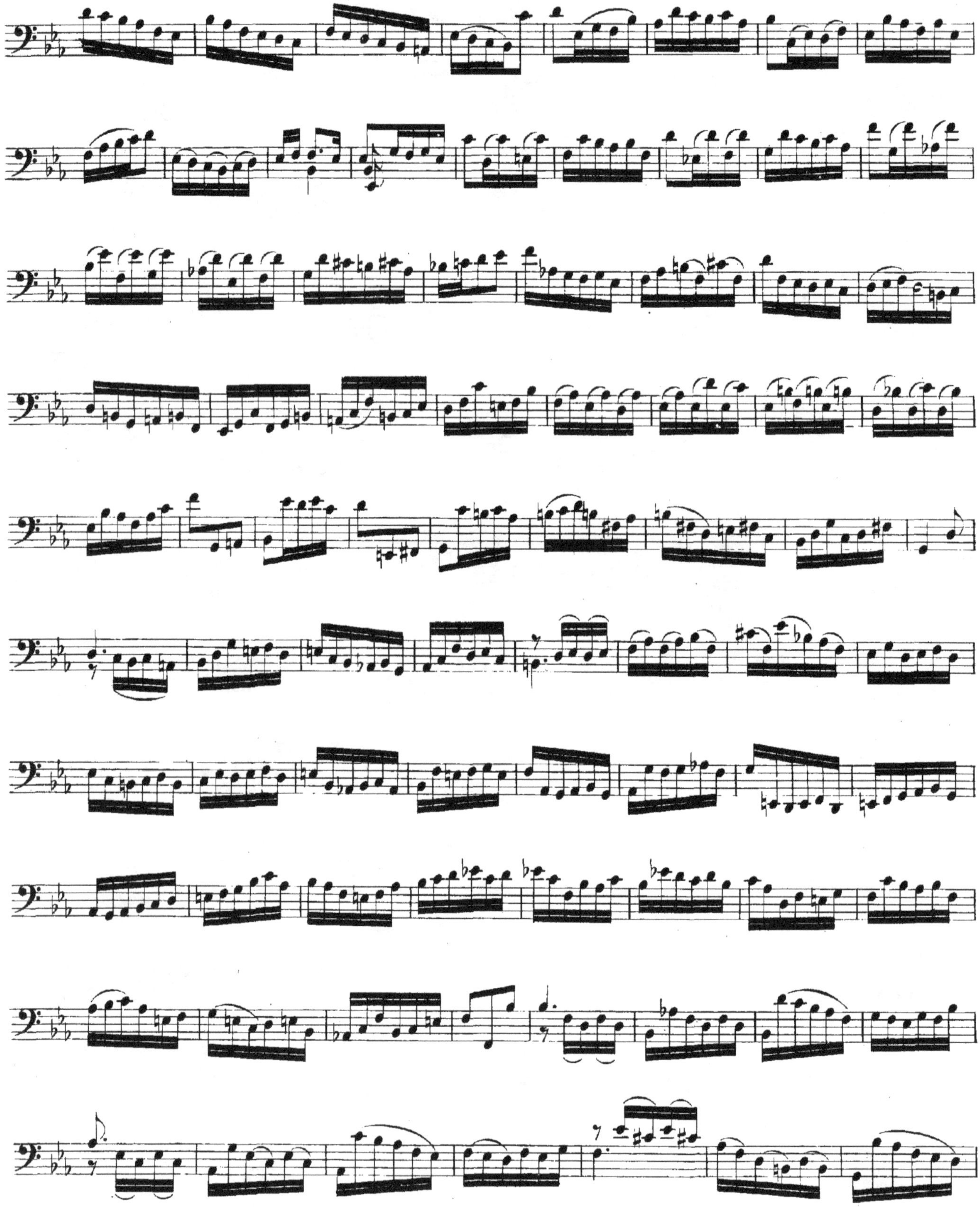

B. W. XXVII.(1)

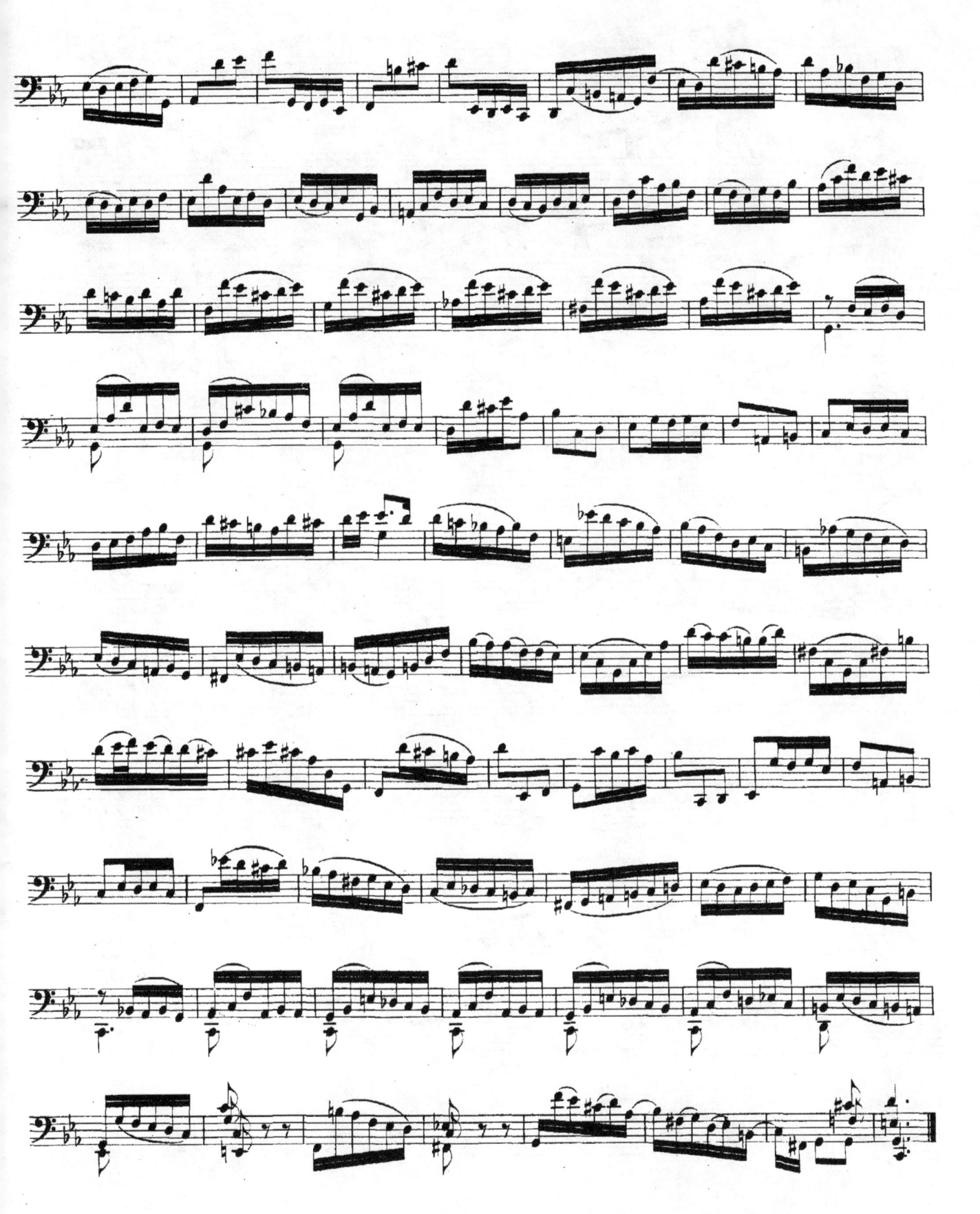

B. W. XXVII. (1)

Allemande.

Courante.

Sarabande.

Gavotte I.

Gavotte II.

Gavotte I. da Capo

Gigue.

SUITE VI.

À cinq cordes, accordées en

Prélude.

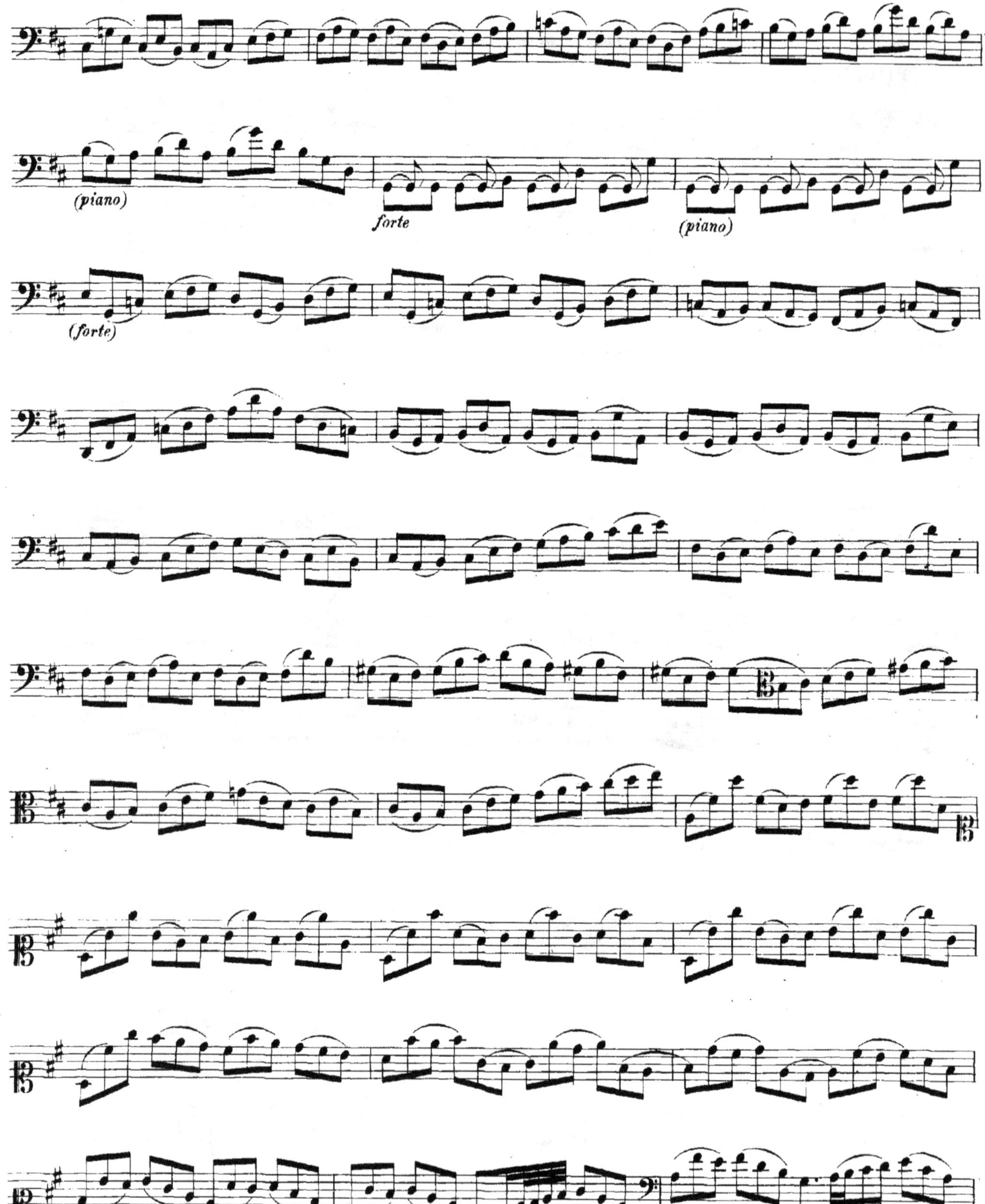
(piano)
forte
(piano)
(forte)

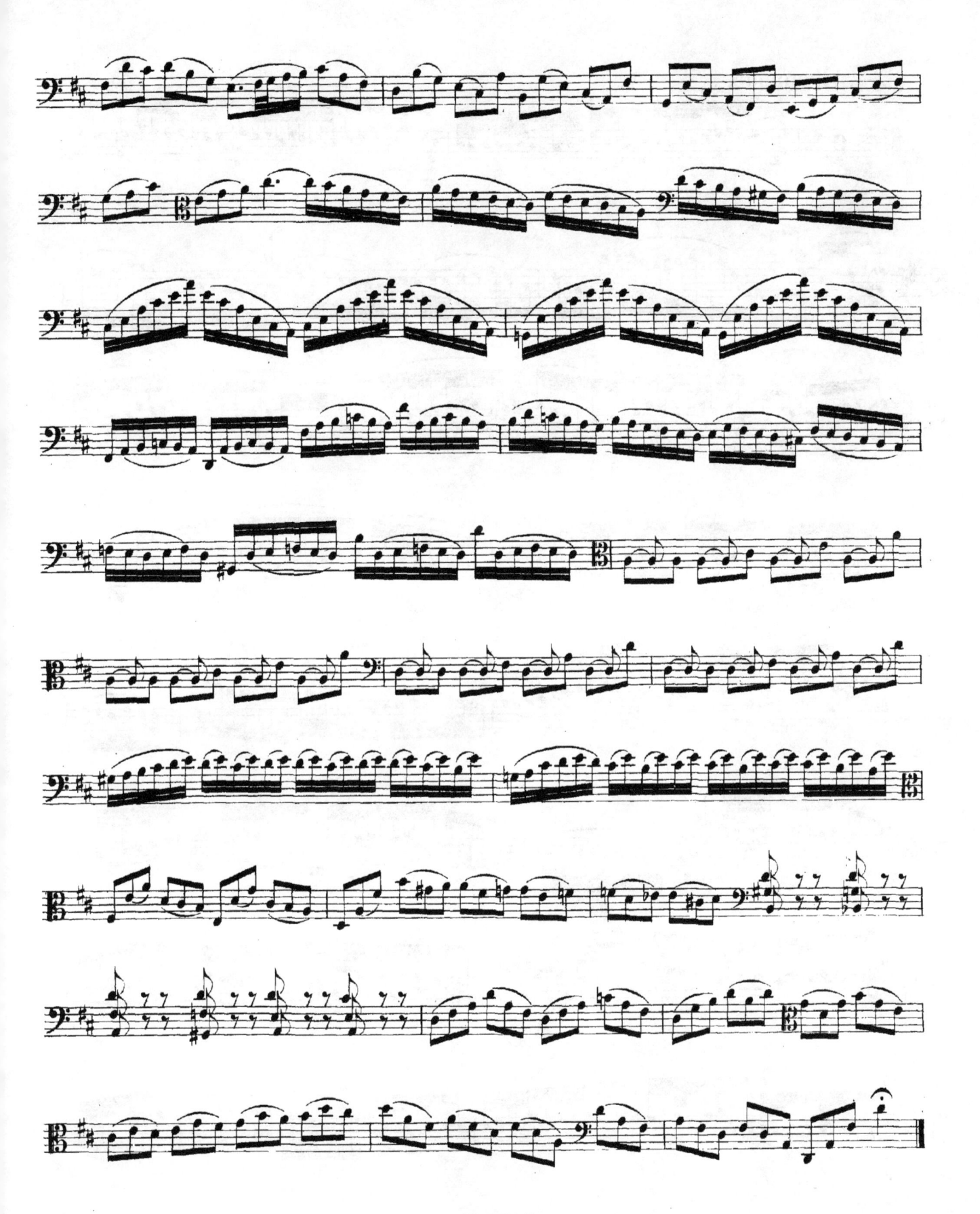

Allemande.

Courante.

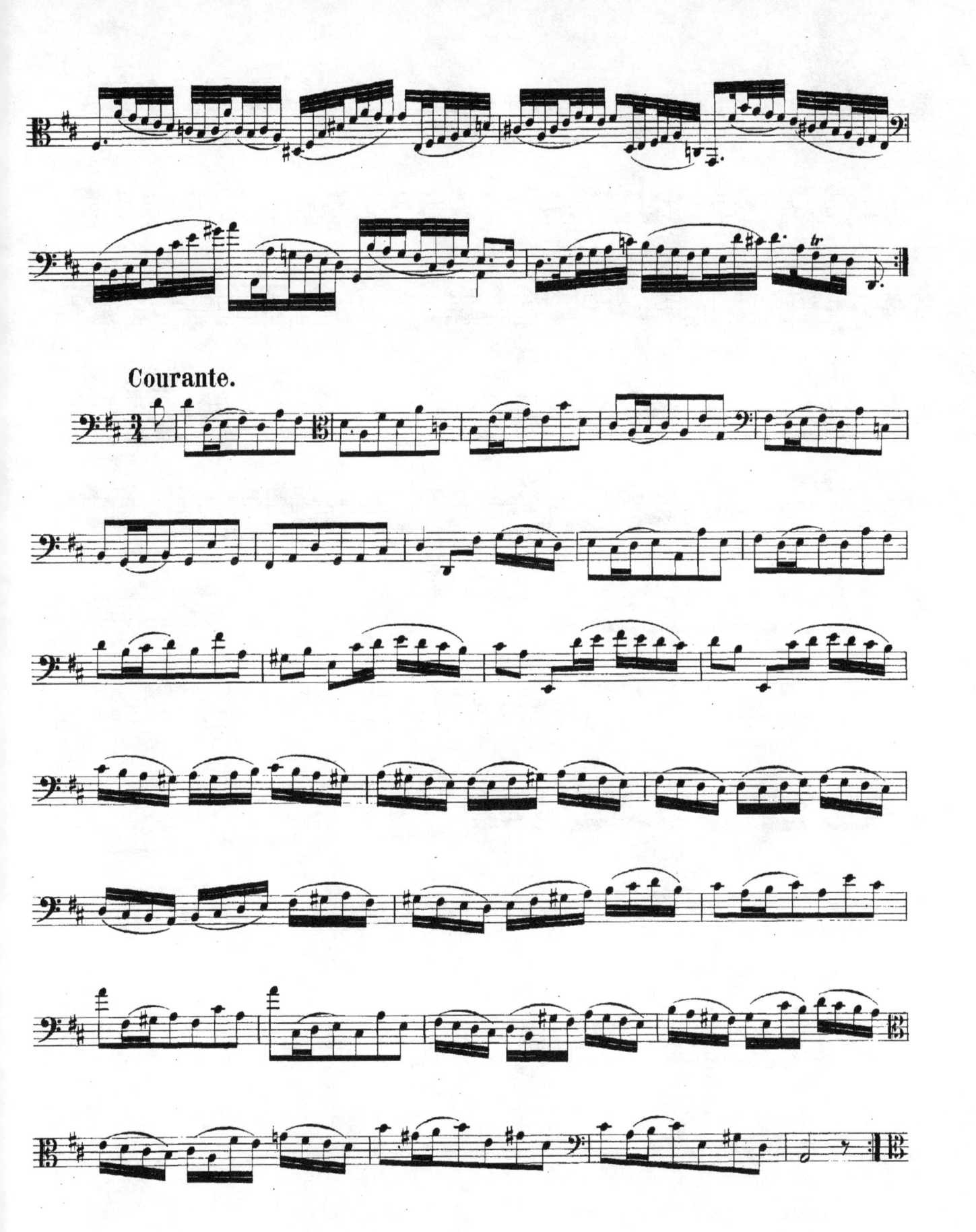

Sarabande.

Gavotte I.

Gavotte II.

Gavotte I. da Capo.

Gigue.

CPSIA information can be obtained
at www.ICGtesting.com
Printed in the USA
BVHW060002100623
665704BV00008B/349